THE
COMPLEAT TURKEY

Shouldn't that be
C-O-M-P-L-E-T-E ?

THE
COMPLEAT

TURKEY

by
Sandra Boynton

Recycled Paper Press

A DIVISION OF
RECYCLED PAPER PRODUCTS, INC.
CHICAGO, ILLINOIS

FIRST EDITION

Library of Congress Cataloging in Publication Data

Boynton, Sandra.
   The compleat turkey.

   SUMMARY: Presents descriptions of the various
"turkeys" of contemporary life in all fields — doctors,
teachers, bureaucrats, politicians — as well as comments
on "turkeys" in general.
   1. Failure (Psychology) — Anecdotes, facetiae, satire,
etc. [1. Wit and humor] I. Title.
PN6231.F28B68   741.5′973   80-17537
ISBN 0-316-10484-1

PRINTED IN THE UNITED STATES OF AMERICA

To whom it may concern

TABLE OF CONTENTS
(Stuffing)

PART II *(continued)*

INTRODUCTION

Who Are the Turkeys and What Do They Want?

They are among us. Now.

There are turkeys in every walk of life. They are in your neighborhood, your school, your business, perhaps *even in your home.*

It is not a pleasant thought.

Of course there are always the skeptics, those self-proclaimed "experts" who say, "An invasion of turkeys? Ridiculous."

An invasion
of turkeys?
Ridiculous.

Don't let yourself be intimidated. You've seen the evidence. You know they're out there.

Just how extensive the turkey infiltration may be is anybody's guess. Some authorities cite estimates of the turkey population that indicate its growth is "epidemic." Others believe that turkeys are simply a "significant minority."

But virtually no one can dispute or ignore these alarming statistics:

- There are more turkeys in politics than in any other profession.

- 75% of all licensed drivers are turkeys.

- Turkeys account for at least half the population of Los Angeles. That's *every other resident.*

And the problem gets worse by the day. Turkeys have two things working in favor of their survival and proliferation:

1. They tend to reproduce themselves;

and 2. There are not only born turkeys, but thousands upon thousands of converts.

WHAT CAN YOU DO?

You cannot write to your Congressman (for obvious reasons). But neither can you sit silently by.

You must take it upon yourself to BECOME INFORMED.

It is the intention of this book to help you do just that. *The Compleat Turkey*—with its authoritative information, comprehensive descriptions, and detailed illustrations—will help you verify suspected turkeys, anticipate their actions, and avoid them whenever possible.

But you must realize at the outset that this book offers no easy solutions. The problem is not going to go away.

PART I
GETTING TO KNOW THEM

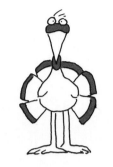  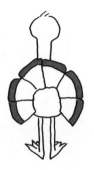 

FRONT VIEW   **SIDE VIEW**   **REAR VIEW**   **BIRD'S-EYE VIEW**

IMPOSTOR

CHAPTER 1
What Is a Turkey?

We all know the old saying, "A turkey is in the eye of the beholder." Or, "Everybody's somebody's turkey."

But are these statements in fact true? Are there no objective criteria, no universal standards to which we can refer in assessing the turkitude of another?

Fortunately, there are. What follows are the five general rules that govern the behavior of turkeys.

RULE NUMBER ONE:

A turkey spends a great deal of time improving others.

RULE NUMBER TWO:

A turkey takes its work very seriously.

Here it is, three full years' worth of work: a complete listing of all your current clients (up to three years ago) arranged in alphabetical order. I decided to list them alphabetically by middle initial in order to protect you from corporate espionage. If you need more than these two thousand copies, just let me know.

RULE NUMBER THREE:

A turkey considers itself exempt from any rules.

RULE NUMBER FOUR:

A turkey's beliefs are determined not by principles but by situation.

RULE NUMBER FIVE:

A turkey never gives up.

Of course, there are as many variations on these five rules as there are turkeys. But there is one constant, one underlying theme: the telltale signs of a turkey are behavioral. Turkey is as turkey does.

CHAPTER 2
A Brief History

The earliest known turkey is Meleagranthropis, followed by Cro-Turgnon and then Neopithetic Turkey.

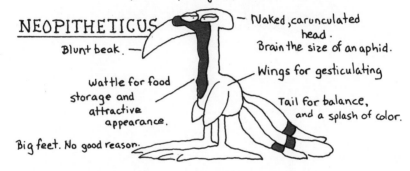

Note vacant expression, still quite evident in modern descendants.

NEOPITHETICUS

Blunt beak. —

— Naked, carunculated head.

Brain the size of an aphid.

Wings for gesticulating

Wattle for food storage and attractive appearance.

Tail for balance, and a splash of color.

Big feet. No good reason.

A while later came the Ancient Turkeys, the most famous of which are chronicled in Pluturch.

VĒNĪ, VĪDĪ, MAƐNĪ, MÃ,
    CACHA TĪGRƐM BAƐDAS TÃ,
IFFĪ HOLLƐRS, LƐDƐM GÃ,
    VĒNĪ, VĪDĪ, MAƐNĪ, MÃ.

Then there were the Dark Ages,

the Middle Ages,

the Renaissance (when just about any turkey could do anything),

and the Enlightenment.

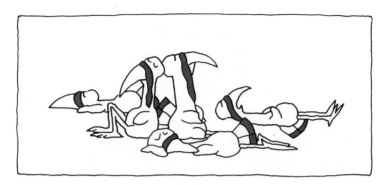

Then came the Industrial Revolution, leading the way to mass production. Thus, by the early part of this century, the work of any one turkey could affect the lives of thousands.

And now, through the advances of modern technology, we have the possibility of almost instantaneous communication and access to information.

The most significant change brought about by the Technological Revolution is in communications. The development of the various media has profoundly affected all our lives: a century ago, you would only have known your local turkeys; today, you come into contact with more turkeys in a single week than you would once have met in an entire lifetime.

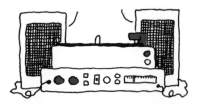

CHAPTER 3
Turkey Chic

Any trend, any movement, any fashion you can name owes much of its popularity to turkeys. This applies to anything from clothes and recreation all the way to philosophical movements.

Turkeys accept any new fashion with great enthusiasm,

and as easily reject old passions.

Once started, a movement will gain many turkey followers simply by virtue of its popularity. Being "current" lends an air of authority to any turkey.

You mean to tell me you've never even BEEN to Adult Roller Disco? Do you realize what you're doing to your biokinesthetic interaction mechanism?

Above all, turkeys thrive in any movement that focuses on self (self-affirmation, self-realization, self-perpetuation, self-involvement, self-basting). The appeal of these movements is that they involve no actual *change* of self.

To summarize: turkeys are of a feather; they flock together, thereby creating mass movements. Mass movements, by their very mass, attract turkeys.

The inevitable question, then—and it is one that has baffled philosophers since time immaterial—is: Which comes first, the turkey or the trend?

CHAPTER 4
Arguing with a Turkey

It is best never to argue with a turkey. Turkeys are absolutely convinced of their intellectual acumen and absolutely incapable of sustaining logical thought. They are therefore fearsome opponents.

But if you must argue, here is how:

1. Present your hypothesis.

I believe that the earth revolves around the sun.

Boy, are you dumb! Everybody knows the sun comes up in the east and goes down in the west.

2. Elaborate your hypothesis.

It is the rotation of the earth that causes that illusion.

Boy, are you dumb! I bet you're an anarchist.

3. Point out your opponent's illogic.

How does that follow?

Boy, THAT'S a typical anarchist comment if I ever heard one!

4. Defend yourself.

I AM NOT AN ANARCHIST!

Boy, I can see you're sensitive about that! Maybe we should discuss this later, when you aren't so overwrought.

5. Review the argument.

6. Retaliate in kind.

TURKEY!

CHAPTER 5
Sense of Humor

Four things characterize the sense of humor of a turkey:

First, it is insensitive.

Second, it is predictable.

Third, it is unwise.

And last, it is nonreciprocal.

PART II
THE PROFESSIONAL TURKEY

Now that you are familiar with the turkey at large, you are ready to learn about turkeys at work.

In Part Two we will examine representative turkeys in the various professions. More compleat information was to be included at the back of this volume, in the form of detailed graphs, tables, and charts. However, professional advice prevailed:

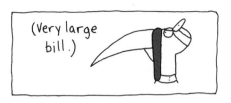

(Very large bill.)

CHAPTER 6
The Turkey as Doctor

There is widespread opinion that all doctors are turkeys. This is not true. There are at least seven or eight exceptions.

The Medical Turkey knows that patients are important — the more, the merrier. The most efficient doctors make no distinction between patients; everyone gets the same treatment. Although this procedure has the desired result (maximizing the number of patients by minimizing the time spent per patient), there can be some unfortunate side effects. Sometimes the doctor's advice may be inappropriate to a particular patient,

You've got to stop smoking.

and sometimes a patient may find the doctor's comments woefully ambiguous.

Many Medical Turkeys deal with patients simply by speaking as succinctly as they write.

CHAPTER 7
The Atturkey-at-Law

Why do you need a lawyer at all? That's a very good question. Let me see if I can clarify that for you.

In the event that the party of the first part (hereinafter sometimes referred to as "you") were to handle your affairs *in pro per* without benefit of a duly engaged legal counsel, you would be subject to numerous difficulties, obstacles, and obstructions.

To wit: the party of the first part so unencumbered of said counsel of a legal nature would be unequipped to manufacture, endure, and/or disentangle the concomitant accumulation of ab hoc legal appropriation of the language.

If you do decide to engage my services, I will consider this a courtesy consultation. If not, cough up seventy smackers.

CHAPTER 8
The Turkey as Professor

In your essay, you failed to consider the <u>human</u> elements of the novel, the dynamic flux between innocence and pathos. You did not adequately deal with the work's central themes: the tyranny of blind hypocrisy, the visionary eloquence of silence. You failed to fully appreciate the essential and ultimate value of compassion. You flunk.

CHAPTER 9

The Insurance Turkey

The turkey in insurance is trained to be a stabilizing influence on clients. When you are content, your agent reminds you of the undercurrent of catastrophe in all our lives.

Supposing, God Forbid, that anything should happen to your car or, God Forbid, your house or even you, God Forbid?

Supposing a terrible tornado hit just two days after you had fractured your wrist in a skiing accident, and while you were trying to clear away some of the considerable debris,

using your one good arm as best you could,

a gang of rotten thieves came and stole your last remaining items of value? Well, we want to be there. We want to take your troubles and make them ours, God Forbid.

And when you are distraught, your agent is a model of serenity.

Mel Gallopavo here... Oh, really? Gee, that's too bad. Anything of valve taken?..Oh, really? Gee, that's too bad. We'll all you need to do is to send us a photograph of the burglar and... You didn't? I'm afraid that makes things more complicated. All right, for now just send us snapshots of all the stolen items and... You don't? Hmmmm. Okay, I tell you what: just have all your bills of sale notarized and send... Well, where are they, then?... It seems to me you're trying to make it as difficult as possible for us to consider your claim.

44

CHAPTER 10
The Turkey Strictly Speaking

← *What does this mean?*

the turkeys.

The turkey as language arbiter is the most hardworking of all. ∧

It is concerned with the preservation of — *that language* *individuals*
~~Its calling is to preserve~~ the language, to save ~~it~~ from those∧who

speak or write ~~(it)~~ casually. *incorrectly* *which language?*

FROM WHAT?

No one is exempt. Every sentence ~~you~~ speak, every paragraph *one*

one *contains* *an abundance* *e usage.* *one* *needs*
~~you~~ write is loaded with ~~horrors~~ of ~~imprecision~~ And ~~you~~ [hardly

barely
~~have to~~ work at ~~(it at all.~~ *examples of*

NOT / what?
A SENTENCE

SHUN THE PASSIVE VOICE!

CHAPTER 11
The Turkey as Psychologist

Turkeys abound in the Social Sciences in general, and in Psychology in particular. Psychology turkeys are committed to proving those things that before, we could only guess at. These are among their most significant findings to date:

1. If you starve a rat for three days, then offer it the choice of food or listening to Beethoven, most rats will choose food. (This finding has led to significant speculation on the importance of aesthetic experience vis-à-vis survival.)

2. Subjects who live in small, dark rooms for four years tend to be more cynical and depressed than those living in spacious homes for the same length of time. (Conclusion based on observation of graduate students in Psychology in Group A, faculty and administration in Group B.)
3. Misery has a love/hate relationship with company.

CHAPTER 12
The Turkey as Politician

... and the PEOPLE are tired of PROMISES! The PEOPLE want a LEADER who can DELIVER. I AM THAT LEADER. And I will FIGHT for your individual RIGHTS and NEEDS because the PEOPLE IS INDIVIDUALS! You and you and you is an individual people, and *you will not be shortchanged any longer.* If you elect ME, I will give you LESS GOVERNMENT and MORE JOBS; I will INCREASE WAGES and REDUCE PRICES. I will build your schools and CUT YOUR TAXES.

Mr. Candidate, I'm curious to know where the revenue for the proposed programs is going to come from.

From the COURAGE and the SPIRIT and the UNQUESTIONING FAITH that have MADE THIS NATION GREAT!

CHAPTER 13
The Turkey Teaching Creative Writing

All right, Class, now I'm going to read you two letters, and I want you to listen carefully and tell me which is the better letter:

Dear Mary,

   I want you to know how much I enjoyed our weekend at the shore. It was a nice change of pace for me, and it was great fun being with you and your family.

                    Thanks a million,
                        Carol

Now here's the second letter:

Dear Mary,

   The billowy waves crashing upon the shore, the plaintive cries of the circling gulls far above our heads, the whoosh and whirr of the sand stirred by angry winds: all these impressions yet linger. Thank you for these cherished memories.

                    With gratitude,
                        Carol

Now I want you to tell me which one is the more effective letter, because of its vivid word choice and attention to detail.

CHAPTER 14
The Bureaucratic Turkey

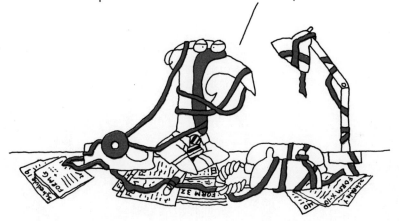

CHAPTER 15
The Corporate Turkey

The turkey in business is often very adept at identifying problems in the company.

And a turkey can always find the perfect solution.

Note: The turkeys won.

CHAPTER 16
The Turkey as Psychiatrist

PART III
TURKEYS AT LEISURE

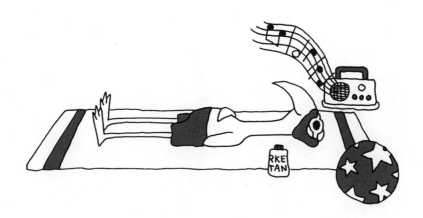

Now we turn to turkeys at play.

Whether playing bingo, snowmobiling, or just plain fooling around, turkeys really know how to enjoy themselves.

EVERYBODY INTO THE POOL!

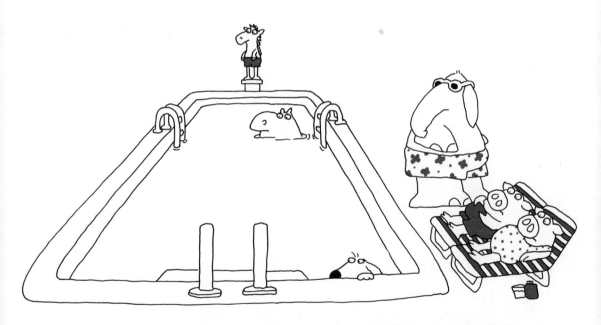

Others may find it more difficult to enjoy them.

CHAPTER 17
At a Party

The turkeys are the ones who arrive early and stay through breakfast. For the most part they try to dominate the party, although there is always one who sits off to the side, complaining to anyone who tries to draw her into the group.

It's all so shallow and meaningless. Don't they realize how rotten things are out there? Doesn't anybody care? I mean, why even have parties anyway?

There is usually at least one turkey who considers himself the life of the party,

> LOOK, EVERYBODY!
> I'M A LAMP!

and another who tries to be the soul of wit.

> ...So I said to the guy, "I'm game."
> Heh heh. GAME. You know, like in
> GAME bird. See, <u>he</u> thought I
> meant that I was willing to
> go along, but actually
> I really <u>am</u> game, being
> a turkey and all. So it
> was a spontaneous pun.
> "I'm game." Heh heh heh...

And a whole group who will at some point get to singing old favorites.

Gradually it might begin to dawn on you that maybe anyone who goes to parties at all is a turkey. But that way madness lies.

CHAPTER 18
Physical Fitness

STRETCHING IT OUT
(40 minutes each side)

Nowadays almost every turkey runs. Most get less mileage out of actual running than out of the fact that they run.

The easiest way to tell a novice turkey runner from a veteran is by vocabulary: beginners use terms such as "second wind" and "runner's high," whereas seasoned joggers are more likely to say things like "shin splints" and "something weird with my left knee."

Of course, not all turkeys run. The turkey who does not want to go to all that trouble gets her exercise by loudly scorning those that do.

JOGGING! HA!
WHAT A WASTE
OF TIME!

Then again, there is always tennis.

CHAPTER 19
The Turkey in Pursuit of Romance

The most remarkable thing about any turkey is its self-confidence. Nowhere is this more remarkable than in the male of the species when his fancy turns to love.

This sublime oblivion well protects the wooing turkey. Often he is very familiar with the dating game, but simply never realizes he is not on the team.

And sometimes, despite careful coaching, he misunderstands the game entirely.

But all turkeys eventually find romance.

CONCLUSION

(Draw your own.)

BOY, I SURE ENJOYED THAT BOOK! IT REALLY NAILED THOSE TURKEYS!